Countries Around the World

Philippines

Michael Burgan

Heinemann Library
Chicago, Illinois

www.capstonepub.com
Visit our website to find out more information about Heinemann-Raintree books.

To order:

☎ Phone 888-454-2279
💻 Visit www.capstonepub.com to browse our catalog and order online.

©2012 Heinemann Library
an imprint of Capstone Global Library, LLC
Chicago, Illinois

Edited by Abby Colich and Claire Throp
Designed by Ryan Frieson and Steven Mead
Original illustrations © Capstone Global Library, Ltd., 2012
Illustrated by Oxford Designers & Illustrators
Picture research by Ruth Blair
Originated by Capstone Global Library, Ltd.
Printed in China by China Translation and Printing Services

15 14 13 12 11
10 9 8 7 6 5 4 3 2 1

Library of Congress Cataloging-in-Publication Data
Burgan, Michael.
 Philippines / Michael Burgan.
  p. cm.—(Countries of the world)
 Includes bibliographical references and index.
 ISBN 978-1-4329-6108-4 (hb)—ISBN 978-1-4329-6134-3 (pb)
1. Philippines—Juvenile literature. I. Title.
DS655.B87 2012
959.9—dc22   2011015436

Acknowledgments

The author and publishers are grateful to the following for permission to reproduce copyright material: Corbis pp. 10 (© Bettmann), 11 (© Christian Kober/Robert Harding World Imagery), 12 (© David H. Wells), 13 (© Romeo Ranoco/ Reuters), 16 (© Dennis M. Sabangan/epa), 21 (© Specialist Stock), 30, 39 (© Rolex dela Pena/epa), 31 (© Reuters); Dreamstime.com pp. 5 (© Simon Hack), 25 (© Simon Gurney); Getty Images pp. 8 (Ted Aljibe/AFP), 17, 22, 28 (Jay Directo/AFP), 26 (Romeo Gacad/AFP), 35 (Lonely Planet Images); iStockphoto pp. 15 (© dejan suc), 24 (© simon gurney);Photolibrary pp. 7 (Tom Cockrem/Ticket), 33 (Emma Gutteridge); Shutterstock pp. 18 (© tubuceo), 46 (© adam. golabek); © USGS p. 20.

Cover photograph of a farmer walking through rice paddies on the mountain slopes of Banaue City, Ifugao Province, Philippines reproduced with permission of Corbis (© John Javellana/Reuters).

We would like to thank Edith R. Borbon for her invaluable help in the preparation of this book.

Contents

Some words in the book are in bold, **like this**. You can find out what they mean by looking in the glossary.

Introducing the Philippines

Can you imagine a country made up of more than 7,000 islands? That country exists in the Pacific Ocean, east of mainland Asia. It is the Philippines, a land famous for its natural beauty, variety of wildlife, and pleasant **tropical** weather. Taken together, its islands cover an area about the size of Nevada.

As an island nation, the Philippines has no land borders with any other countries. Its closest neighbors are Malaysia (to the southwest), Indonesia (to the south), and China and Taiwan (to the north). The Philippines is a part of a region called Southeast Asia.

An island people

The people of the Philippines, called **Filipinos**, live on fewer than half of the islands that make up their nation. Most of the islands cover less than 1 square mile (2.6 square kilometers). Many islands don't even have names. The largest island is Luzon. Manila, the nation's capital, is located there. To the south is the large island of Mindanao. In between is a group of smaller islands called the Visayas.

Different backgrounds, one nation

The Philippines today is a blend of several distinct **cultures**. The first settlers were **Malay**. Spain then controlled the islands for several hundred years. The United States ruled the Philippines for a time, as did Japan during World War II. The Filipinos were finally granted their independence in 1946. Filipinos reflect these different influences. Many have Southeast Asian roots, Spanish names, and speak English. But at heart, the people know they are a distinct nation, and they are proud to be Filipino.

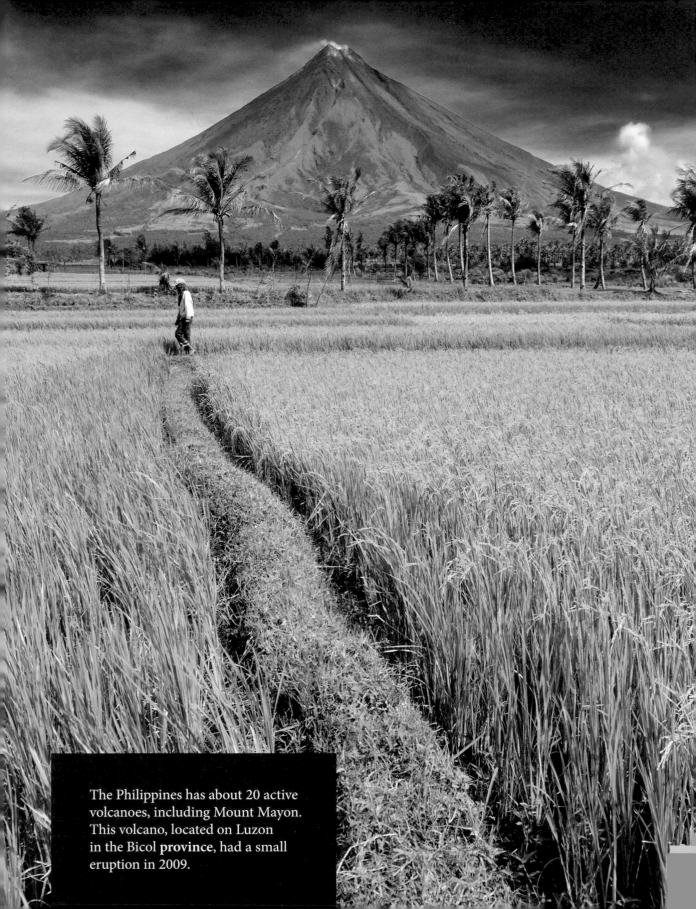

The Philippines has about 20 active volcanoes, including Mount Mayon. This volcano, located on Luzon in the Bicol **province**, had a small eruption in 2009.

History: Path to Independence

At least 50,000 years ago, humans came to the Philippines from Indonesia or other nearby lands. They arrived on rafts and made their homes in caves. The newcomers hunted wild animals and gathered wild fruits and vegetables for their food.

Starting about 3000 BCE, people began sailing to the Philippines from parts of China and what are now Malaysia and Indonesia. People formed villages called *barangays*. The leader of each one was called a *datu*.

The appearance of Islam

Over the centuries, **Filipinos** traded with other people from distant lands. These included **Arabs**, who began sailing to the Philippines in the 1200s. The Arabs brought their faith, **Islam**, to some southern Philippine islands. Small **Muslim** kingdoms soon spread across the region, mainly on Mindanao.

The Spanish arrive

In the late 1400s CE, Spain began sending ships around the world. The kingdom wanted to trade cloth and jewels for valuable spices and metals. In April 1521, Portuguese explorer Ferdinand Magellan made an agreement with the Spanish king to gain support for a new expedition. He reached the Philippines and landed on the island of Cebu, in the Visayas. He convinced the local *datu* to become a **Roman Catholic**. Other **tribes** rebelled against Magellan and the *datu*, and Magellan was killed. But the remaining sailors returned to Spain, completing the first sea voyage around the world.

In 1565 **conquistador** Miguel López de Legazpi brought the first Spanish settlers to the Philippines. He called the islands *Las Filipinas*, in honor of Spain's king (spelled *Philip* in English). The Spaniards built a fort on Cebu. By 1571 the Spanish had made Manila, on Luzon, the capital of their new Asian **colony**.

Miguel López de Legazpi began building Fort San Pedro soon after he arrived in Cebu. Visitors can explore the remains of the fort and a small museum inside its gate.

Ships called **galleons**, such as this one, carried goods between Manila, China, and Mexico during the years 1565 to 1815.

Life under Spain

At times, the Filipinos fought the Spanish. The Muslim Filipinos living in the south, on Mindanao, were organized enough to resist the invaders. But Luzon and the surrounding islands came under Spanish control. The Spanish began using the Philippines as a base for trade. By the end of the 1500s, the Philippines was the key link in the first international trade between the Americas, Europe, and Asia.

Religion and society

The Spanish brought their Roman Catholic faith to the Philippines. Many Filipinos adopted this religion. The Spanish also forced Filipinos to work for them and pay taxes. The Spanish let some local Philippine leaders keep their power, as long as they were loyal to Spain. Chinese merchants were important in the Philippines, organizing trade with China.

Some Spanish men married Chinese or Filipino women. Their children were called **mestizos** if they were male and **mestizas** if they were female. They played key roles in local affairs. By the late 1800s, many mestizos and mestizas were well-educated and wealthy. But the Spanish and Roman Catholic priests still controlled the government.

A fight for independence

By the 1890s, many Filipinos wanted independence from Spain. A revolution began in 1896. The Filipinos greatly outnumbered Spanish troops. The fighting ended late in 1897, with the Spanish still in control.

ANDRES BONIFACIO (1863–1897)

Andres Bonifacio came from a poor family. Although he did not have much schooling, Bonifacio was able to read, and by the 1890s he became convinced the Philippines should receive their independence from Spain. He led a revolution in 1896, but was killed by fellow rebels who disagreed with him over how to fight the revolution. Filipinos consider Bonifacio a national hero.

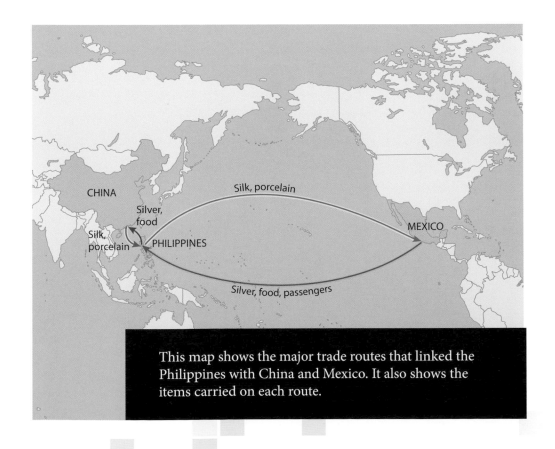

This map shows the major trade routes that linked the Philippines with China and Mexico. It also shows the items carried on each route.

The Americans arrive

In April 1898 Spain and the United States went to war, and the Americans quickly won. As a result, they took control of the Philippines by buying it from Spain for $20 million. Former rebels there also challenged the new U.S. rule. During the fighting that followed, as many as 22,000 Filipino soldiers and 600,000 **civilians** died. The United States won this bloody war (sometimes known as the Philippine War of Independence) in 1902.

The Americans began building hospitals, roads, and schools. They created a government that let the people make some of their own laws. But the Americans also made young Filipinos study English, not their native languages. The history of the Philippines was also largely ignored.

In June 1898, Filipinos led by Emilio Aguinaldo declared independence from Spain. But the country soon came under U.S. control.

Independence at last

In December 1941, during World War II (1939–1945), Japan invaded the Philippines. U.S. and Filipino troops fought side-by-side. Many were killed on the Bataan Death March, when the Japanese forced thousands of troops to march long distances. Japan controlled the islands until early 1945.

The Americans and their **allies** finally defeated Japan. U.S. leaders kept an earlier promise to grant the Philippines independence. On July 4, 1946, Filipinos finally had their own nation.

These children sit on a jeepney used in the countryside.

Daily Life

Starting in 1945, U.S. soldiers left vehicles called jeeps in the Philippines. Filipinos took parts from the jeeps and other vehicles to create larger, open-sided buses called jeepneys. Brightly painted and decorated, they are still used today in public transportation, alongside buses.

Problems after independence

After independence, small groups of people controlled most of the power and wealth in the Philippines. In 1953 Ramon Magsaysay was elected president. He tried to help the poor by creating new jobs. In 1957 he died in a plane crash. The presidents who ruled after him were not as concerned about average Filipinos.

The Marcos years

Ferdinand Marcos was elected president in 1965. He ruled as a **dictator**. His wife, Imelda, angered people by spending large amounts of money on herself, while many Filipinos faced **poverty**. For many years, Marcos arrested people who challenged his rule. One of them was Benigno "Ninoy" Aquino, Jr., a popular politician. In 1983 Aquino was killed by a government soldier.

Massive groups of people gathered to oppose Ferdinand Marcos and support Corazon Aquino.

Aquino and beyond

During the 1986 presidential election, hundreds of thousands of people filled the streets to protest Marcos' rule. The People Power, or EDSA, Revolution was peaceful—people even brought their families. Most people supported Aquino's wife, Corazon, to replace Marcos as president. She won the vote.

But since Corazon Aquino left office in 1992, the country has struggled at times. Several presidents have broken the law or misused their power. The country still has many poor people. In 2002, **terrorists** in the south tried to create an independent Muslim nation. But in 2010, newly elected president Benigno "Noynoy" Aquino III—the son of Corazon Aquino and Benigno Aquino, Jr.—said he would work hard to build a stronger Philippines.

CORAZON AQUINO
(1933-2009)

Corazon "Cory" Aquino was widely loved. As president, she helped restore some of the political rights Ferdinand Marcos had taken away.

Regions and Resources: Mountains and More

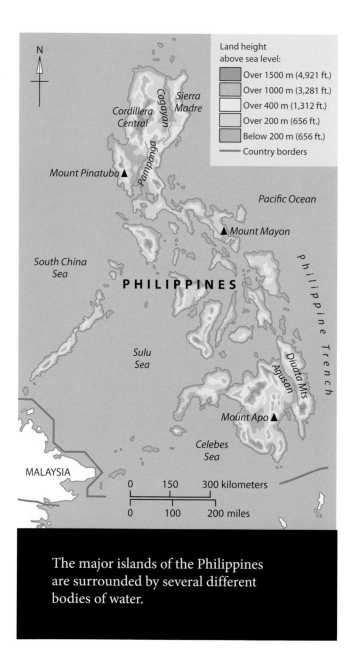

Land height above sea level:

- Over 1500 m (4,921 ft.)
- Over 1000 m (3,281 ft.)
- Over 400 m (1,312 ft.)
- Over 200 m (656 ft.)
- Below 200 m (656 ft.)
- —— Country borders

Sierra Madre

Cordillera Central

Cagayan

Pampanga

Mount Pinatubo ▲

Pacific Ocean

▲ Mount Mayon

South China Sea

PHILIPPINES

Philippine Trench

Sulu Sea

Diuata Mts

Agusan

Mount Apo ▲

Celebes Sea

MALAYSIA

| 0 | 150 | 300 kilometers |
| 0 | 100 | 200 miles |

The major islands of the Philippines are surrounded by several different bodies of water.

Of the 7,107 islands in the Philippines, the largest is Luzon, at 40,541 square miles (105,000 square kilometers). Luzon has the tallest mountain range in the country, the Cordillera Central. Some of its peaks reach over 9,000 feet (2,743 meters). Luzon is also the site of the largest and most important Philippine city, Metro Manila. Metro Manila is made up of 17 distinct cities, with a total population of more than 11.5 million people in 2010. *Intramuros*, the Old Spanish part of the city, has some buildings that date back to the late 1500s.

Region of many islands

The Visayas make up the middle part of the Philippines, where there are hundreds of islands. The largest include Samar, Cebu, Leyte, Negros, and Panay.

Each of these has a major mountain range, with some peaks more than 8,000 feet (2,438 meters) tall. The region produces a wide range of crops, especially sugar cane and rice, along with corn, coconuts, and bananas. Fishing is another important part of the **economy**.

Island of the south

Mindanao is the second-largest island in the Philippines, and the heart of its southern region. It covers 39,399 square miles (102,043 square kilometers). The country's highest point, the active volcano Mount Apo, is located here. Off its east coast is one of the deepest spots in the world, the Philippine **Trench**. It is 34,578 feet (10,593 meters) deep.

Rice is often grown on flat spaces of land, called terraces, cut into hills and mountains.

Tropical weather

The Philippines is known for its pleasant, warm climate. Across the country, temperatures rarely go below 81°F (27°C), though some mountain cities see temperatures fall much lower. **Monsoons**, or strong winds, bring heavy rains during some months, and dry air during others. This gives the country distinct wet and dry seasons.

YOUNG PEOPLE

When a typhoon is near, charity groups such as Save the Children help **Filipino** children that are caught in the typhoon's path. Some children and their families receive food and medical supplies. Others are moved to shelters far from the storm's path.

These Filipinos had their homes destroyed by Typhoon Megi, which struck Luzon in 2010.

This Filipino man is returning home with shrimp caught in traps.

Some leading exports

Food	Sales, US$ (Jan.–Oct. 2010)
Coconut products	1.8 billion
Fish	276 million
Bananas	254 million

Manufactured goods	Sales, US$ (Jan.–Oct. 2010)
Electronic products	26.5 billion
Machinery/ transportation equipment	2.2 billion
Garments	1.4 billion

Source: www.census.gov.ph/data/sectordata/2010/ex101002a.htm

Deadly storms

Tropical weather can lead to deadly storms called **typhoons**. Typhoons are also called hurricanes. They often strike the Philippines between June and December. Typhoons can have winds of over 150 miles (241 kilometers) per hour and produce high tides along the coast. In 2010 Typhoon Megi killed at least 27 people and destroyed 200,000 homes.

Natural resources

The different regions of the Philippines produce valuable resources. Many of them are **exported**. Coconut oil is used around the world in cooking, and it is one of the country's top food exports. Filipinos also harvest trees that are used for lumber, paper, and other items. Fish are another important resource, whether caught in seas or raised in lakes and fish farms. The Philippines also produces important minerals, such as gold, silver, iron, nickel, and copper.

Wildlife: Rare and Unusual

Cut off from the rest of Asia, the islands of the Philippines have wildlife found nowhere else on Earth. High in the mountains and deep in the **rain forests**, scientists are still discovering new **species** of animals.

Animals of all kinds

The Philippines has plenty of common animals, such as deer, mice, monkeys, and squirrels. But there are also many that are unique to the Philippines, including the *kagwang*, or flying lemur. The animal doesn't really fly. It glides from tree to tree in the forest, using flaps of skin to catch the wind. Another rare creature is the Palawan bearcat.

Many whale sharks swim in the waters off Donsol, on the island of Luzon.

There are over 200 different kinds of reptile, including the Philippine crocodile. It is shorter than other crocodiles and usually lives in freshwater.

Favorite flowers

The Philippines has more than 13,000 plant species, and perhaps half of the species are found nowhere else on Earth. The Philippines is famous for orchids—hundreds of kinds grow there. One native species, the waling-waling, is called the Queen of All Orchids. The country's national flower is the Arabian jasmine, locally known as *sampaguita*. **Filipinos** sometimes string the flowers together to create necklaces called leis. Another well-known flower, the ilang-ilang, is used to make perfumes.

New discoveries

One of the new animals recently found in the Philippines is the hairy-tailed rat. This rat lives on Mindanao. Another new animal is the Camiguin hanging parrot. Residents of the island of Camiguin sometimes keep these birds as pets.

How to say...

In the Filipino language, *butanding* (boo-tan-deeng) refers to the whale shark, often called the gentle giant of the seas. It is the world's largest fish, reaching up to 66 feet (20 meters) long. Tourists in the Philippines sometimes swim alongside these gigantic sea creatures.

Both wildlife and people are threatened when a volcano erupts, as Mount Pinatubo did in 1991.

Wildlife in danger

Forests once covered the Philippines. But in the last 60 years or so, more than half have been cut down. Some trees are cut for wood, while others are cleared so crops can be grown. This has affected local wildlife. Across the Philippines, more than half the species of wildlife could become **extinct**.

The danger is especially high in Philippine rain forests. They are home to many of the country's thousands of species of plants and animals. One of these is the Philippine eagle, the country's national bird. This large, rare eagle used to live all over the Philippines. Now it is found only on small parts of Luzon and Mindanao.

Cutting down the forests leads to other problems. The trees help remove the gas **carbon dioxide** from the air. This gas plays a part in **global warming**, which is a rise in temperatures across Earth. Fewer trees means there is more harmful carbon dioxide in the air.

Some solutions

The Philippine government has created more than 200 areas to protect trees and other wildlife from human activity. There are 71 national parks and **reserves**, including Tubbataha Reefs Natural Park. In recent years, the populations of some nearly extinct species have been rising.

YOUNG PEOPLE

In many Luzon schools, Project EcoKids teaches young people how to reduce the production of carbon dioxide and other harmful gases. The children use colorful books and put on plays to show what they have learned.

A variety of sea life live along the Philippine reefs, such as these at Apo Reef National Park.

Infrastructure: Building a Modern Nation

In 1987 **Filipinos** created a new **constitution** that is still used today. The Philippines is a **republic**—voters elect people to represent their interests. The Philippine system is based on the government of the United States.

The national government

The Philippine national government has three distinct branches, or parts. Laws are created in Congress, which has two parts—the House of Representatives and the Senate.

REGIE SAHALI-GENERALE

Men have controlled politics in Muslim Mindanao (ARMM) for several decades. But a woman, Regie Sahali-Generale, has made history by winning important political positions. In 2010 she was chosen as vice-governor of the ARMM, the second-most-powerful position in the government there.

The House of Representatives meets in Quezon City, in the Metro Manila region.

The executive branch, led by the president, makes sure the laws are carried out. This branch has departments that handle issues such as education, foreign affairs, and the military. The third branch is the judiciary, or court system. The courts decide if people accused of breaking the law are innocent or guilty.

Regional and local governments

The Philippines is divided into 17 regions. These are divided into 80 **provinces**, and both regions and provinces have elected government officials, as do cities, towns, and the smallest political unit, the *barangay*. The country has tens of thousands of these villages.

Two regions in the Philippines are considered distinct. In northern Luzon, many native peoples live in the Cordillera Administrative Region. Many of them seek greater independence from the national government in Manila. In the south, the Autonomous Region in **Muslim** Mindanao (ARMM) has been granted some independence to run its own affairs.

Several regions in the Philippines have 16 cities, including the National Capital Region (Metro Manila). Region VIII, Eastern Visayas, has more than 4,300 *barangays*—more than any other region.

Map labels: N; 0 150 300 kilometers; 0 100 200 miles; CAGAYAN VALLEY; ILOCOS; Luzon; CENTRAL LUZON; ■Manila; Pacific Ocean; SOUTHERN TAGALOG; BICOL; Mindoro; South China Sea; Samar; PHILIPPINES; Panay; EASTERN VISAYAS; Leyte; WESTERN VISAYAS; Palawan; CENTRAL VISAYAS; Sulu Sea; Negros; NORTHERN MINDANAO; Mindanao; WESTERN MINDANAO; CENTRAL MINDANAO; SOUTHERN MINDANAO; Celebes Sea; MALAYSIA

Building a healthy nation

The Philippine government has many concerns, including health care. President Benigno Aquino III hopes to provide medical care for the poorest Filipinos. Large cities have good medical care, with well-trained doctors and nurses. However, because of their great skill, Filipino nurses often find good jobs in other countries.

Daily Life

While many Filipinos rely on modern transportation, some still use traditional forms. A *banca* is a type of boat called an **outrigger**. *Bancas* have been used in the Philippines for hundreds of years. Some new models have motors, while others have sails or are rowed by oars. *Bancas* are usually taken for short journeys between small islands.

Newer *bancas* are made out of metal instead of wood and can carry up to 50 passengers.

Metro Manila has both modern buildings and ones hundreds of years old. The tallest is the Golden Empire Tower, at 666 feet (203 meters), which was completed in 2002.

Building a healthy economy

The government also plays a role in business and transportation. In recent years, the government has provided money for banks. Some national banks then lend money to **industries** and farmers. The Philippine **currency**, or money, is called the peso.

To move goods and people easily, the government builds roads and airports. Ships and boats of all sizes are also important in an island nation. The country's major ports are in Manila, Batangas, and Limay, in Bataan Province.

Manila is also home to the country's largest airport, Ninoy Aquino International Airport. In 2005 a new airport opened in Pampanga, on what used to be a U.S. military airfield. The country has recently spent money to improve its railroads. Roads for vehicles, however, are often not in good shape. Fewer than half of the country's roads are paved.

Education

One of the Philippine government's main roles is to educate its citizens. The government provides each person with up to 10 years of free public schooling. Children must enter elementary school at age six, and they must attend for at least six years. (Some children attend private schools, often starting at age five.) About half of the students then go on to four years of secondary (high) school (see the chart at right). In 2010 the government proposed a new plan to add two more years to public schooling.

The Philippine government hopes to give students more experience with computers.

Education statistics, 2008–2009

	Elementary	Secondary
Number of schools (public and private)	44,691	10,066
Number of students	13.7 million	6.8 million
Number of teachers	405,588	193,224
Percentage of students completing program	73.2	75.2

Source: UNESCO and the Department of Education of the Philippines

YOUNG PEOPLE

The school year begins in June and runs until April. In the younger grades, students take classes in both English and Filipino, which is based on the main native language, **Tagalog**. In later years, almost all classes are held in English. In special schools for Muslims, called *madrasahs*, students also learn Arabic and the teachings of their religion.

After high school, at about age 16, students can go to one of about 1,000 colleges, universities, or vocational schools (schools that teach skills for particular jobs). The University of the Philippines is the only national university, with campuses in different cities across the country. It has about 50,000 students. The oldest university, the University of Santo Tomas, was founded in 1611 by the Dominican Order of the **Roman Catholic** Church. The Dominicans continue to run it to this day.

Culture: A Blend of Peoples

Filipinos sometimes refer to themselves and their **culture** as *Pinoy*. *Pinoy* culture reflects the influence of the native Asian peoples, the Spanish, and the Americans.

All types of music

Some early Filipinos sang most of their songs without any instruments playing along. Today, many Filipinos listen to and create music influenced by **Western** pop stars. In some areas, they still sing traditional songs, such as love songs called *kundiman*. A form of music called Original Pinoy Music features pop songs sung in Filipino or other native languages.

Dancing is also popular, with some dances tracing their roots to Spanish, **Muslim**, and native cultures. One of these is the *singkil*, a Muslim dance, which is performed during festivals. Another example is the *tinikling*, a fast-paced dance in which dancers hop, skip, and step over bamboo poles.

Filipino men wear the white, lightweight *barong* for many occasions.

The written word

The official language of the Philippines is called Filipino. It is based on one of the major native languages of the country, **Tagalog**. People sometimes also use the word "Tagalog" to refer to the Filipino language.

Before the Spanish arrived, Filipinos had several alphabets they used for writing. The first great Filipino writers, however, did not emerge until the 1800s. José Rizal is a national hero who wrote poems and novels. He wanted independence from Spain. During the 1900s, José Garcia Villa was a widely praised poet. In recent years, F. Sionil José has won praise for his novels, which are written in English. Other writers use Filipino or other native languages.

Main languages of the Philippines

Language	Number of speakers
Filipino (Tagalog)	22,000,000
Cebuano	20,000,000
Ilocano	7,700,000
Hiligaynon	7,000,000
Bicolano	4,800,000
Waray-Waray	3,100,000
Kapampangan	2,900,000

Art of the people

Filipinos are proud of the many kinds of native, or folk, art found on the islands. Examples include items handmade from colorful beads and different metals, as well as **textiles**. Many Filipinos still wear traditional clothes for special events.

A girl dances in a religious festival called the Ati-Atihan, which is held each January in the town of Kalibo.

Religious life

The **Roman Catholic** faith has shaped religion in the Philippines for more than 400 years. Yet some people blend old practices and beliefs with the Catholic teachings. For example, a ceremony called the *pasyon*, held during Holy Week (before Easter), has its roots in the old faiths.

In recent years, some Christian Filipinos have moved away from Catholic teachings. The country has two Christian churches that were developed there: the Aglipayan Christian Church and the Iglesia ni Cristo (Church of Christ). In the south, **Islam** remains strong.

Festivals and celebrations

Many Philippine holidays and celebrations are based on the Catholic religion. Most towns have a party, or *fiesta*, to honor a saint. These are open to everyone not just the people who live in the town. The *fiesta* can last for three days. In some towns, part of the *fiesta* takes place on the water, as the image of the local saint is placed on a boat.

Other holidays are tied to important historical events and people. February 25 marks the end of Ferdinand Marcos' rule, and June 12 is Independence Day. November 1 is All Saints' Day. November 2 is All Souls' Day, when families visit the graves of dead relatives. Christmas is celebrated for weeks.

YOUNG PEOPLE

At many festivals, Filipino children take part in a game called *pabitin*. Baskets filled with candies or toys are hung from a bamboo rack. The children reach for the baskets, while an adult raises and lowers the rack.

Tacloban, on Leyte, is the site of the colorful Kasadyann festival, which shows how people of the region adapted to Christianity while keeping some of their own dress and culture.

The best of Philippine food

No festival is complete without food, and Filipinos have some favorites for these special events. *Lechon*, or a whole roast pig, is the center of festive meals. Rice is a part of most meals, and other common ingredients include coconut, fish, garlic, and ginger. Milk from the native water buffalo is sometimes used to make cheese. This is called *kesong puti*, which means "white cheese." It is wrapped in banana leaves. *Suman* is sweet rice wrapped in banana leaves and steamed. Each region has a slightly different version of this dish.

Filipinos at play

Popular sports in the Philippines include boxing, mixed martial arts, and ping-pong (table tennis). People who can afford the equipment enjoy water sports, such as snorkeling and scuba diving. Pool, or billiards, has become more common in recent years. Basketball is the most popular team sport while many enjoy playing badminton. Kite-flying is popular as well, with some fliers competing in international contests.

MANNY PACQUIAO (BORN 1978)

Manny "Pacman" Pacquiao is one of the greatest boxers of all time. He has won championships at eight different weight limits. He has brought great pride to his country—and he generously shares the wealth he makes from boxing, aiding victims of **typhoons**. In 2010, while still pursuing his sport, Pacquiao was elected to serve in the Philippine Congress.

Palitaw

Try making these sweet rice cakes as a snack or dessert.

Ingredients

1 cup sweet rice flour

$^3/_4$ cup water

$^1/_2$ cup coconut flakes

$1^1/_2$ cups white powdered sugar

$^1/_4$ cup sesame seeds

What to do

1. Mix together the sweet rice flour and water.

2. Cover your hands in flour, and then shape the dough into egg-size ovals. Flatten with your thumb.

3. Boil water in a saucepan. (Have an adult help you use the stove.)

4. Drop palitaw in boiling water.

5. Scoop out with a slotted spoon as soon as the ovals float. Leave to cool slightly.

6. Roll in grated coconut.

7. Serve the sweet rice cakes with the sugar mixed with toasted sesame seeds.

The Philippines Today

Filipinos are famous for their warm welcome to guests. Tourists quickly see this kindness. Several million tourists visit the Philippines each year, and the number is rising. Visitors also see the country's great natural beauty. The government promotes tourism as a way to create jobs and improve the **economy**.

Building a stronger country

The effort to create jobs is key for the Philippines. The population is rising, and many people live in **poverty**, especially in the cities. About one-third of the country gets by on just $1 per day. In 2010 the country won praise for new rules that made it easier to create businesses and to trade overseas. The economy is also helped by money sent from Filipinos working overseas, known as OFWs (overseas foreign workers). In 2008 more than eight million Filipinos had jobs in other countries.

President Benigno Aquino III wants to improve how the government is run. In the past, it was filled with **corruption**—officials expected to be paid money to approve certain projects, or they favored their friends and relatives over other people. The thirst for political power has also led to violence. Government corruption and political violence have kept companies away. Aquino sees ending corruption as a way to improve his country's economy.

Looking ahead

The Philippines is a unique blend of **Malay** and **Western cultures**. It has natural resources the world wants, as well as people who are willing to work hard. Philippine leaders believe the country can overcome its problems and provide a better life for all its citizens.

In the near future, the
government hopes to attract up
to six million tourists a year to
the Philippines.

Fact File

Official name: **Republic** of the Philippines

Nationality: Filipino

Languages: **Filipino** and English (official), variety of native languages also spoken, including Cebuano and Kapampangan

Capital city: Manila

Population: 99.9 million (2010 est.)

Largest cities (populations): Metro Manila (11.55 million)
Davao City (1.36 million)
Cebu City (800,000)

CALOOCAN CITY

VALENZUELA

NAVATOS   MALABON   QUEZON

CALOOCAN   MARIKINA

SAN JUAN

MANILA   MANDALUYONG

PASIG

Manila Bay   MAKATI

PASAY   TAGUIG

PATEROS

PARANAQUE

LAS PINAS

MUNTINLUPA

Laguna de Bay

N

0   5   10 kilometers

0   5 miles

By population, Quezon City is the largest of the 17 cities in the National Capital Region, with more than 2.7 million people.

System of government: Republic

Date of independence: July 4, 1946 (from the United States); earlier date of declared independence from Spain is celebrated as Independence Day—June 12, 1898

Major religions: **Roman Catholic**, **Muslim**, Evangelical Protestant, Iglesia ni Cristo, Aglipayan, other Christian groups

Life expectancy: 71.3 years

Literacy rate: 92.6 percent

Climate: **Tropical** with a rainy **monsoon** season from June to October; drier monsoons from December to February; typhoons common from July to November

Area (total): 117,187 square miles (300,000 square kilometers)

Coastline: 22,554 miles (36,289 kilometers)

Major rivers: Cayagan, Pulangi, Agusan, Pampanga, Pasig

Major volcanoes: Mount Mayon, Taal Volcano, Mount Apo

Highest elevation: Mount Apo, 9,692 feet (2,954 meters)

Lowest elevation: Philippine Sea, 0 feet (0 meters)

Natural resources: Minerals, forest products, food products, and fishery products

Local currency: Peso

Major industries: Electronic components, **textiles** and clothing, food processing, pharmaceuticals, chemicals, machinery and equipment, transportation equipment, electronics and semiconductor assembly, mineral products, hydrocarbon products, fishing

Imports: Electronic products, mineral fuels, machinery and transportation equipment, iron and steel, textile fabrics, grains, chemicals, plastic

Exports: Semiconductors and electronic products, transportation equipment, garments, copper products, petroleum (oil) products, coconut oil, fruits

National flower: Sampaguita (Arabian jasmine)

National tree: Narra

National fruit: Mango

National bird: Philippine eagle

National fish: Bangus (milkfish)

National animal: Kalabaw (carabao)

Famous Filipinos: Andres Bonifacio (1863–1897), leader of a revolt against the Spanish
Benigno Aquino (1933–1983), political leader
Benigno Aquino III (born 1960), president
Corazon Aquino (1933–2009), first woman president
Ferdinand Marcos (1917–1989), president

President Benigno Aquino III is known by the nickname "Noynoy."

Gabriela Silang (1731–1763), first Filipino woman leader of a rebellion

Imelda Marcos (born 1929), wife of Ferdinand Marcos

José Rizal (1861–1896), writer, political leader

Manny Pacquiao (born 1978), boxer and politician

National anthem
"Lupang Hinirang" ("Chosen Land")

Land of the morning
Child of the sun returning
With fervor burning
Thee do our souls adore.

Land dear and holy,
Cradle of noble heroes,
Ne'er shall invaders
Trample thy sacred shores.

Ever within thy skies and through thy clouds
And o'er thy hills and seas;
Do we behold thy radiance, feel the throb
Of glorious liberty.

Thy banner dear to all hearts
Its sun and stars alright,
Oh, never shall its shining fields
Be dimmed by tyrants' might.

Timeline

BCE means Before the Common Era. When this appears after a date, it refers to the number of years before the Christian religion began. BCE dates are always counted backward.

CE means Common Era. When this appears after a date, it refers to the time after the Christian religion began.

BCE

| 50,000 or earlier | People live in caves across the Philippines. |
| 300 | Settlers arrive from China and other parts of Asia. |

CE

1200s	**Muslim** traders begin appearing in the region.
1521	Ferdinand Magellan lands on Cebu.
1565	Miguel López de Legazpi brings the first Spanish settlers to the Philippines.
1571	Manila becomes the main Spanish port and center of government.
1896	**Filipinos** begin a war for independence from Spain, led by first José Rizal and then Andres Bonifacio.
1898	Filipinos declare their independence from Spain; the United States wins the Spanish-American War and takes control of the Philippines; war begins between U.S. troops and Filipino rebels.
1902	Fighting between the Filipinos and Americans ends.
1916	The Jones Law calls for the Philippines' independence from the United States at some future date.
1935	Filipinos write their own **constitution** and begin to run their own government.

1941	Japan invades the Philippines during World War II.
1945	World War II ends, and the Japanese leave the islands.
1946	The Philippines gains independence.
1953	Ramon Magsaysay is elected president and tries to improve the lives of average Filipinos.
1965	Ferdinand Marcos is elected president.
1972	Marcos introduces a new constitution giving him almost complete power.
1983	Marcos' political opponent, Benigno Aquino Jr., is murdered.
1986	After mass protests, Marcos flees the country; Corazon Aquino becomes president.
1987	Filipinos approve a new constitution, making the country a **republic**.
1991	A major eruption of the volcano Mount Pinatubo forces thousands of people from their homes.
2002	Philippine and U.S. troops pursue **terrorists** in the southern part of the country.
2009	Violence breaks out during local elections in Mindanao.
2010	Benigno Aquino III is elected president and promises to end **corruption**.

Glossary

ally person or nation that works with another one, particularly during wartime

Arab person whose roots are in part of the world known as Arabia, which lies between the Red Sea and the Persian Gulf

BCE meaning "before the common era." When this appears after a date, it refers to the time before the Christian religion began. BCE dates are always counted backward.

carbon dioxide gas produced when people and animals breathe out and when certain fuels are burned

CE meaning "common era." When this appears after a date, it refers to the time after the Christian religion began.

civilian person who is not a member of the military

colony area ruled by another country

conquistador warrior and explorer who claimed new lands for Spain

constitution system of laws and principles that govern a nation or state

corruption dishonest or illegal behavior or misuse of power

culture practices, beliefs, and traditions of a society

currency bills and coins accepted in return for goods and services

dictator ruler with absolute power over the people

economy having to do with the money, industries, and jobs in a country

export to ship goods to other countries for sale or exchange

extinct no longer found on Earth

Filipino name for the people and the language, which is based on Tagalog

galleon large sailing ship once used by the Spanish government

global warming slow rise in Earth's temperature, partially caused by human activity

industry companies that make goods or provide services

Islam religion founded in Saudi Arabia during the 600s CE based on the teachings of Muhammad

Malay person whose roots are in a part of Asia that includes parts of Malaysia and Thailand

mestizo/mestiza man/woman with parents from different racial or ethnic backgrounds

monsoon season of heavy rains

Muslim person who practices Islam or something related to that religion

outrigger boat with beams connected to a separate floating device that helps the boat stay balanced

poverty extreme lack of money

province specific region within a country

rain forest tropical forest with dense growth and high annual rainfall

republic independent country with a head of government who is not a king or queen

reserve area set aside to protect wildlife

Roman Catholic Christian who belongs to the church of the same name, which is based in Rome and headed by the pope

species particular type of animal or plant

Tagalog main native language of the Philippines on which the Filipino language is based

terrorist person who uses random violence to create fear in order to achieve some larger goal

textile clothing or other item made out of cloth

trench deep hole in the ground

tribe independent social group

tropical hot and humid

typhoon powerful storm that forms over tropical waters in parts of the Pacific Ocean; in other regions it is called a hurricane or tropical cyclone

Western relating to European nations and other countries, such as the United States and Australia, with similar political systems and cultures

Find Out More

Books

Baker, Stuart. *In the Tropics (Climate Change)*. New York: Marshall Cavendish Benchmark, 2010.

Ganeri, Anita. *Eruption! The Story of Volcanoes*. New York: Dorling Kindersley, 2010.

Gordon, Matthew. *Islam (Understanding Religions)*. New York: Rosen, 2010.

Schraff, Anne E. *Philippines (Country Explorers)*. Minneapolis: Lerner, 2009.

Skog, Jason. *Teens in the Philippines (Global Connections)*. Minneapolis: Compass Point, 2009.

Websites

https://www.cia.gov/library/publications/the-world-factbook/index.html

Find out more by reading the CIA World Factbook entry on the Philippines.

www.seasite.niu.edu./Tagalog/Tagalog_mainpage.htm

This website from Northern Illinois University is designed to teach Tagalog, but it also has information about Philippine culture and history.

www.congress.gov.ph/download/13th/studentguide_2004.pdf

For information on the Philippine Congress, check out this website that is written for children.

http://news.bbc.co.uk/2/hi/asia-pacific/country_profiles/1262783.stm

Learn more about the Philippines on this BBC web page.

www.philtourism.com/

See some of the top tourist sites in the Philippines on the official tourism website.

Places to visit

If you are lucky enough to visit the Philippines, here are some of the places you could visit:

San Agustin Church, Manila

Built in 1587, San Agustin Church contains the tomb of Miguel López de Legazpi, the Spanish explorer who became the first governor of the Philippines.

St. Paul's Subterranean National Park, Palawan

St. Paul's Subterranean National Park has the world's longest underground river. Visitors can explore it by boat.

Samal Island, off Davao

Samal Island has many fine beaches and deep caves for exploring.

Topic Tools

You can use these topic tools for your school projects. Trace the flag and map on to a sheet of paper, using the thick black outlines to guide you. Then color in your pictures. Make sure you use the right colors for the flag!

The national flag of the Philippines has a white triangle of equal sides with a yellow sun in the center. The equal sides represent the equality of all people, and the eight rays of the sun stand for the eight provinces that rebelled against the Spaniards. In each corner of the triangle is a star representing Luzon, Visayas, and Mindanao. One blue and one red stripe are next to the triangle. The blue stands for peace and unity, and the red represents the blood Filipinos have shed to defend their country. During wartime, the flag is flown with the red stripe on top. Otherwise, the blue is on top.

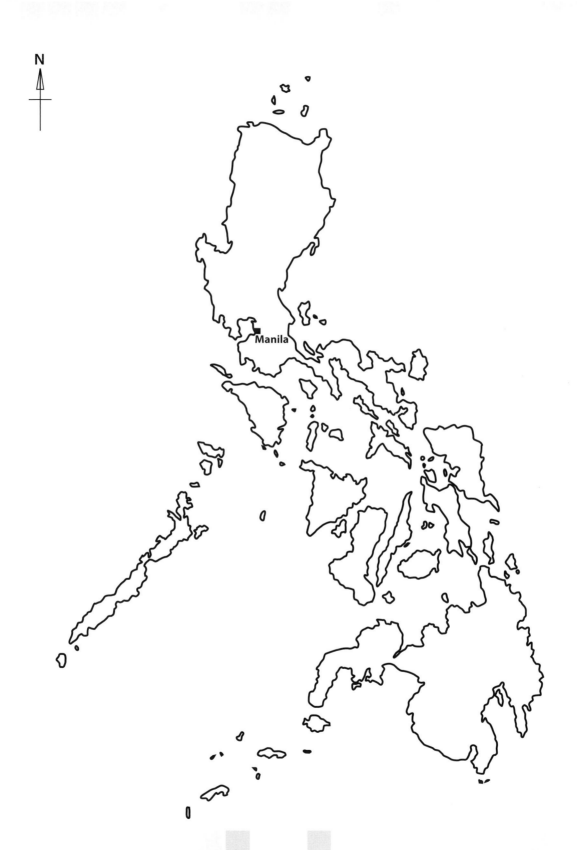

N

Manila

Index

Titles in the series

Afghanistan	978 1 4329 5195 5	Japan	978 1 4329 6102 2
Algeria	978 1 4329 6093 3	Latvia	978 1 4329 5211 2
Australia	978 1 4329 6094 0	Liberia	978 1 4329 6103 9
Brazil	978 1 4329 5196 2	Libya	978 1 4329 6104 6
Canada	978 1 4329 6095 7	Lithuania	978 1 4329 5212 9
Chile	978 1 4329 5197 9	Mexico	978 1 4329 5213 6
China	978 1 4329 6096 4	Morocco	978 1 4329 6105 3
Costa Rica	978 1 4329 5198 6	New Zealand	978 1 4329 6106 0
Cuba	978 1 4329 5199 3	North Korea	978 1 4329 6107 7
Czech Republic	978 1 4329 5200 6	Pakistan	978 1 4329 5214 3
Egypt	978 1 4329 6097 1	Philippines	978 1 4329 6108 4
England	978 1 4329 5201 3	Poland	978 1 4329 5215 0
Estonia	978 1 4329 5202 0	Portugal	978 1 4329 6109 1
France	978 1 4329 5203 7	Russia	978 1 4329 6110 7
Germany	978 1 4329 5204 4	Scotland	978 1 4329 5216 7
Greece	978 1 4329 6098 8	South Africa	978 1 4329 6112 1
Haiti	978 1 4329 5205 1	South Korea	978 1 4329 6113 8
Hungary	978 1 4329 5206 8	Spain	978 1 4329 6111 4
Iceland	978 1 4329 6099 5	Tunisia	978 1 4329 6114 5
India	978 1 4329 5207 5	United States of America	978 1 4329 6115 2
Iran	978 1 4329 5208 2	Vietnam	978 1 4329 6116 9
Iraq	978 1 4329 5209 9	Wales	978 1 4329 5217 4
Ireland	978 1 4329 6100 8	Yemen	978 1 4329 5218 1
Israel	978 1 4329 6101 5		
Italy	978 1 4329 5210 5		